SIMPLY
SELF-SUSTAINED

Your guide to living the independent,
self-sufficient life that you desire.

BRIANNA HOWELL

Welcome, and thank you for choosing Simply Self-Sustained as part of your life's journey!

Learning to live a self-sustained life is a very personal and individual decision. Your reasons can be very different from another for wanting this lifestyle, as well as how deeply you want to delve into self-sufficient living. Whether you are looking to simply change a small area of your life, such as growing your own vegetables, or a more drastic change in several areas, there are some basics that will help guide you.

Simply Self-Sustained is here to help prepare you for your journey to the independent life you desire. Simply Self-Sustained will cover the basics of getting started. Where to start, organization, schedules, care and maintenance, budgeting, and much more, so welcome, and let's get started!

• TABLE OF CONTENTS •

•ONE•

THE BASICS

Welcome to Simply Self-Sustained. In this chapter, we will cover the basics of living an independent, self-sustained life. This chapter is designed to give you the very basic information you need to know and understand, to make your entry into self-sustained living a success.

Starting Small

Firstly, start small. Decide on what you want to accomplish and start small. If you want to grow your own vegetables then pick one and get to know it. If you want to change several areas of your life, I encourage you to make a list in order of importance and start at the top, but start small.

Much of your journey is going to consist of research. Research your project. Learn what you need and what potential problems may occur.

If you want tomatoes, raising chickens, or crafting, that's great, but start small. Pick one craft and get good at it. Start with five or six tomato plants. Care for them and see how much harvest you get off of those five or six plants before splurging for a dozen. Buy two or three hens and learn them. How much food do they need? How many eggs do they lay? You may be surprised at how many eggs you have, or find that you need more.

Whatever you choose, start small. Take the time to get comfortable with your choice. Learn as much as you can, get good at it, and find ways to become more efficient at it.

Some will tell you to 'Master' your choice, but I don't think that's really fair. Self-Sustained living doesn't necessarily mean 'mastering' anything. I've been doing this for decades and still learn new things every day or how to become more efficient. It is more important to become familiar and comfortable with your project than to 'Master' it. When you are familiar with what you are working with, you learn to recognize what is normal versus what is not.

If you see black spots on your tomato plant leaves, you may not be able to diagnose and cure them immediately, but you are comfortable enough to know that is not normal. That is what is most important. Go about your business, then when you have a moment, go research and find the cure. If you are dealing with live animals, I would recommend making the research a priority or calling your vet, but the key here is to know enough to recognize what's normal and healthy and what is not.

Start small, and above all, be patient with yourself! You are going to make mistakes. There, I said it! You are going to make mistakes! Do not be discouraged or disheartened by this, just know that it's a fact, and keep trying. Mistakes do happen, but they are just ways of teaching us how not to do something, and now you know.

This is the biggest reason for starting small. Mistakes. If you go all out right away and things don't work out, you could be out hundreds of dollars or more. If you buy a dozen hens, build their coop, buy their food and they don't lay eggs. Not only are you out all of the money you've spent, but you will still be buying your eggs to feed your family.

Start small and keep trying. You will find the best way, that suits your life. Finding your own way cannot be stressed enough. One common trait among people who want a self-sustained life is that they want a life on their terms, but everyone's terms are different, so you need to organize them based on your needs and schedule.

Organization

Living a self-sustained life takes discipline and organization. The larger you go, the more disciplined and organized you need to be. Nobody's life is the same. Schedules are different, climates are different, needs are different, and let's face it, sometimes life just gets in the way. This is your best life you are designing, so design it as closely as you can to your desires and capabilities.

I encourage you to sit back and imagine the life you desire. Your very best day. What time do you want to wake up every day? What time do you want to go to bed every night? Walk through your entire day from waking up, until bedtime. How do you want your self-sustained life to be? Do you want to water your garden in the morning or evening? Yes, there are chores we would love to not have to do, but if you fit them into your best life, they become a choice, not work, so remember to put them into your vision.

As an example, I wake almost every day at 6:00 am, but I like my mornings to be very leisurely. I get up and have a cup of coffee (or two) and go over my day; what needs to be done or appointments I may have. I wander through my kitchen and look out the windows, watching the sunrise and taking time to appreciate everything I have and the goals I'm working towards. I make a quick breakfast, shower and then I'm ready to start my day. By this time, it's about 8:00ish.

Mornings essentially are 'me time'. 'Me time' is very important, but maybe yours is lunchtime or after the kids have gone to bed. Everybody is different and it's okay that your schedule is not the same as somebody else.

The important thing about designing your best life is consistency. Some things are very flexible but others are not. If you are growing a garden or crafting, those are very flexible. You must schedule them into your day, but it doesn't matter when. If you are raising animals, however, that is a very different story.

Animals are flexible in a sense, but very routine. When you get animals and start feeding them at 8:00 am every morning or 6:00 pm, in the evening, they get to know when feeding time is and if you waver from that, they can get very noisy and demanding.

Animals are very forgiving though, so when life gets in the way and feeding is late, while they may have been noisy, the minute you come with the food, life is calm again and all is forgiven. Do not beat yourself up about this! Routine is best for animals in their production and growth, but they do get over the occasional change-up.

Again, animals are flexible to a certain extent. If your schedule changes, so will theirs, but don't worry. You may have a noisy hen house for two or three days, but they are adaptable and will adjust. I change my feeding schedule every winter and spring. Food provides an animal's body heat for warmth, so when freezing starts, I like to give them a later evening feeding to keep them warm overnight. When the weather warms again, I go back to their normal feeding schedule.

Some projects take some TLC each day, while other projects only need care two or three times a week. Do the kids have soccer practice or games? Maybe you need to water the garden a little earlier or later on those days. Do you take a vacation every year? Have a backup plan. Just be sure that when you design your life and start living your self-sustained life, you consider everything to ensure you can give your best to your best life.

The Back-Up Plan

Prepare for the worst; Hope for the best.

Maya Angelou

Not that I advocate pessimism, but living an independent, self-sustained life does mean that you have to prepare for the worst. The first rule in having a backup plan is to never invest more than you have to lose. Drought happens and you don't get the vegetable harvest you expected. Crafts don't sell, or hens don't lay eggs. It does happen and when that happens, not only are you out of the investment you made, but you also have to cover the loss of their production. This means you will have to pay to replace those resources. You will have to buy your vegetables or eggs. If your crafts don't sell, you'll have to cover that loss of income. Do not invest more than you have to lose.

I once bought five ducks for $50 and while I got some eggs from them, I did not predict a weasel getting to them that winter. Not only did I lose my beautiful ducks, but my $50, the money for their food, and any future egg production they would have provided. Now I was back to buying eggs. $50 was a comfortable place for me to start and still be comfortable with the potential loss. Your budget may be different and that's okay. I just want you to be prepared.

The upside is, once you've been doing this for a while, you will have better knowledge of how much you need to accomplish your goals. This means you will expand accordingly and build up a surplus for those unforeseen situations.

You also can't be expected to be home at all times. People like to camp or take vacations. Have a backup plan. Have a friend or family member that you can count on to cover your absence. Walk them through what you need from them and how to do it. Keep it simple for them. If your animals need vaccination on the weekend you're planning to be gone, do it before you leave or when you get home. Do not overwhelm them and remember to show your gratitude. If they are watering your garden, put a basket of vegetables together, to thank them.

The Simply Self-Sustained series will cover all areas of self-sustained living to prepare you to live your best life and I am honored to guide you.

•TWO•

GETTING ORGANIZED

Living a self-sustained life is different for each individual, but again, the one common trait everybody has in their independent life is living life on their terms. This is the life you choose, your best life, on your terms. In this chapter we will cover how to get your life organized, to stay organized, stress-free, and enjoyable. Nothing is without its issues or problems, but this is your best life you're designing, so make it fun, relaxing, and as stress-free as possible!

Learning to live a self-sustained life starts with organization or reorganization. The best way to do this is with organizers or planners. Multiple annual planners are going to become your best friend in staying organized. You can buy these or make them free, online, but as you start or expand on your journey to independent living, you will find them invaluable.

When I started my self-sustained life, decades ago, I went through every area of my life, organizing and reorganizing everything to keep life simple. This is not necessary for everybody, but I felt I needed to organize and compartmentalize each area of my life so that one area didn't suffer in place of another.

Your planner can be as detailed as you wish, but there are some things you will want to make sure to have in them. You will want to have a monthly calendar where you can note the occasional things.

Also, a daily calendar that you can list the regular things that you need to do. Keep a 'Grocery List' in each planner to quickly note any supplies you may be running low on and keep a 'Contact List' for important numbers, especially if you are dealing with animals.

I also keep a 'Project' section in my planner for things that come up outside of regular projects. If a gate latch is broken or I decide to add some flower boxes to the fence, they go in the project section. There is no right or wrong way to set up your planner, as long as you know how to work with it.

When I started living my self-sustained life, I started with tomatoes, and I had one planner for my tomatoes. It only had a monthly calendar and a 'Grocery List'. I did my research on raising tomatoes; their care, potential diseases, and what I would need to care for them. I noted in my monthly planner when to plant, how often to give them extra feed, and their expected harvest date. I also scheduled days to weed and water. Then I went through all of my gardening supplies and put together what I already had. In my 'Grocery List', I noted everything that I didn't have so that I would remember to pick them up in town.

This was a very basic planner for a very basic start, but as I've been doing this for a while now, and my self-sustaining projects have multiplied, so have my planners and their setup. I now have dozens of planners throughout the buildings on my farm and I find they keep me on track and don't allow me to forget even the most minor detail in caring for my farm.

To give you an idea of how to use planners in staying organized, here are some examples of how I use my planners.

The most important planner in my home is the Emergency planner. It is the grab-and-go, in case of emergency, bible. In this planner, I have all of my contact phone numbers. Doctors, my family's numbers, our vet, emergency contact persons, etc.

I also keep a section for each family member with a copy of their social security number, birth certificate, insurance cards, medications, donor or DNR forms, and anything else pertinent to emergency care.

This planner is bright red, clearly and boldly labeled, and kept with the phone book. Everybody in my family knows where it is and how to use it if there is ever an emergency. It's great for babysitters to know as well. Whether you are planning a self-sustained life or not, I highly encourage everybody to have one of these planners.

Next, I have my Everyday planner that goes with me everywhere. In that planner, I have a monthly calendar that I use to keep track of appointments, meetings, kids' school or athletic events, and other things that I need to do, outside of tending to my home. I also have a 'Contacts' section in there, with all of my contact numbers, similar to my Emergency planner.

I also keep a 'Grocery List' section in my Everyday planner, where I transfer all of my other planner's lists to. My Everyday planner is the only one I have when I'm on the go, so before I leave, I go around to the other planners that have a 'Grocery List' section and add them to my Everyday planner. Remember to cross them off your other lists so you don't duplicate them needlessly.

I have a 'Project' section for things that I want to do and what I need for them. This section is a want, not need section, so if the budget allows or I'm in the area, I may pick up what I need for the project, but if not, I can live without it for a while longer.

Finally, I keep a 'Notes' section in this planner. This is for things that I may just need to jot down, or questions I need to ask that I don't want to forget.

In my house, I have a Home Care planner. Yes, it's a House Cleaning planner. Again, it keeps me on track without forgetting the minor things.

In my Home Care planner, I have a monthly calendar where I note the uncommon things that need to be done like washing the curtains or cleaning the oven. I also have daily schedules for what needs to be cleaned each day. I do not love cleaning my house, but I find if I just schedule a couple of things each day, it's not so terrible. Remember, this lifestyle is supposed to be enjoyable!

An Example of my daily cleaning is Tuesdays I dust, everything. Fridays, I sweep, mop and vacuum my floors. If I do these things every week, the dust and dirt doesn't build up so they tend to be fairly quick jobs. When you let them go, things build up and it becomes more time-consuming and more like work than caring for your home.

I have a planner in my home for Houseplants. This planner, I have designed scrapbook style. When I get a new plant, I take the little stick out of it that has its general information, put it on a pretty piece of paper, do some quick research on it, and add notes to the page. Then I decorate it a bit, and viola, I have most of the info I need to care for that plant. I do have an annual monthly calendar in my Houseplant planner so that I can keep track of and schedule any feedings or repotting that my plants may need and of course. A 'Grocery List', but really, that's all that is to it.

Again, you can set your planner up any way you wish, as long as you have the information you need and you know how to use it.

In my garage, I have a planner for my vehicles. My Vehicle planner is divided up by every vehicle from my daily driver to my tractor and lawnmower. This planner has a monthly calendar to note when maintenance was done or needs to be done on that vehicle. I note things like oil changes and tire rotations or new tires or belts, etc, on that calendar. I also keep all of the paperwork and titles in that planner.

I have a 'Contact' section in that planner so that when I'm tending to them, I can quickly look up the number if I need to schedule any appointments. I also keep the trusty 'Grocery List' in that planner, in case I am running low on any supplies I need for them. I also have a 'Seasonal' section in this planner for things like changing to snow tires or changing my lawnmower blades.

I have planners for all of my animals, my barn, my outdoor and greenhouse plant care, seasonal care for my entire farm, and more. I schedule when to plant, when to harvest, when to prune, when to feed and what to feed, vaccinations, and anything else I need to care for. Not only are these planners important for your organization, but they are priceless if you are having somebody watch your home while you are gone. They may not need all of the information you keep, but they will have all they need in one place.

You also need to manage these planners. Things change and need to be added or removed, seasons change and feedings need to be adjusted, and so on. You also have the trusty 'Grocery List' in each planner that needs to be tracked. Plan to make time in your schedule to manage these.

For me, I tend to have Sundays as a pretty relaxed, get ready for my week kind of day. I put aside about an hour on Sunday to go through my planners, update if needed and condense my 'Grocery Lists' into my Everyday planner.

I also note any other things that need to be done such as vet appointments or the HVAC guy coming to service the furnace.

Now that you are getting the idea of how I section and use each of my planners, you can start making a list of the planners you feel you may need to keep for yourself.

Again, design these for you. If you feel you only need a daily planner, that's perfect for you. If you want to add a sales section to your craft planner, then add it. As long as it's manageable for you, then it will help keep you on track. Do keep in mind that these are not meant to create more work for you, they are designed to help keep you organized. While setting up the planners may take some time, overall, these planners are meant to be a reference to keep you on track.

As you design your planners and are making your first 'Grocery List' of supplies you will need, Organize your areas as well. If you are raising chickens, have all of their feed, bedding, tools, and supplies in one place for easy access in your daily tending. The same for each of your animals, gardens, or other work areas. Not only is your organization in your planners but in your daily movement as well. If you feel you need to have more of one thing in different areas, then plan for that.

I have several pitchforks and shovels all over my farm. I have four pitchforks in my barn alone. One for mucking my horse and cow stalls, one for my chicken coop bedding, one for my goat bedding, and one for hay. It's easier for me to have one in each area than running all over looking for the one single pitchfork I have on the farm.

Keeping things organized will not only keep you on track but will make your day flow so much easier, saving you time and aggravation. Another area that will save time and aggravation in your day is 'Keeping it Clean'.

•THREE•

KEEPING IT CLEAN

From your house to your barn, this chapter is dedicated to cleaning without being overwhelmed by it! Housecleaning or mucking stalls are regular things that need to be done and can become daunting when left to do all in one day or weekend. I am going to help you take housecleaning to home care by taking some of the work out of it.

Personally, I prefer to think of housecleaning as home care. A house is just a building and doesn't elicit any feelings or emotions, but when you think of your home, there are feelings of warmth and love, family, pride, friends gathering, and so on, so care for it well. When you are vacuuming or dusting, just remember, you are caring for your home to keep it beautiful because you deserve to live in beauty.

I have never been a great housecleaner but since I started getting organized and using my planner, it doesn't feel like work. I don't come into the house thinking what a mess it is anymore and, best of all, my home is always presentable to anybody who drops by unexpectedly. Using my planner also allows me time to clean those areas that I never had time to do before. Dusting was always a quick, superficial thing, oftentimes done with a shirt sleeve. Now I dust with intent and I dust everything...even my window trim.

The first thing you need to do is reprogram your thinking from housecleaning to home care. Put some thought into what you are doing. You've worked hard to have a home and deserve to have a home you love to walk into at the end of the day. Make it shine! Put your love into it when you take care of it.

Next, make a list of all of your regular home care tasks. Laundry, vacuuming...Everything you can think of that you do regularly. Now add the things that you don't regularly do but know you should or that are only done once in a while like washing the windows or curtains.

Once you have your list, next to each item, I want you to note approximately how long it takes to complete each task. I do not include things like laundry or oven cleaning in this, as the oven takes care of most of the work and the washer & dryer do most of my laundry work. These types of tasks I start, then do other tasks while they're running.

Also, if you have 'mop the floors' on your list, but most of your house is tile and hardwood that would take several hours to do, consider breaking this down by upstairs/downstairs or by room. Optimally, you want most of your tasks to be 15-30 minutes. Now, I want you to break your list down by the frequency of each task. What needs to be done weekly, bi-weekly, monthly, or seasonally.

Your list is now compiled, so it's time to build your home care schedule. A couple of things to keep in mind when building your schedule. One, keep it small. Keep daily home care to 60-90 minutes a day. Remember this is supposed to be enjoyable. Caring for your home. Two, combine similar tasks. If you are washing the windows, wash your curtains at the same time. Go around the house and take down the curtains and put them in the washer. While they are washing, go back and wash the windows. By the time you're done washing windows, the curtains are done and ready to re-hang.

A little tip from me to you; most curtains can be hung wet and air dry, saving time and money. Do the same with laundry. Put your laundry in the washer then go vacuum while the washer is running. Transfer to the dryer and go do another task.

A few more tips from me to you, to reduce your home care list.

One of the things to keep off of your list are the daily tasks. Things like dishes do not need to be on your home care list, as this should be done routinely as part of mealtime.

If you hate water spots on windows, mirrors, and fixtures, use a water repellent on them. You will need to add this to your seasonal home care, but it will make your weekly tasks so much easier. I use water repellent on the outside of my windows, on my mirrors, on all of my faucets and shower doors. Mineral deposits and soap scum don't build up, making them easier to clean.

Keep cleaning products in each room. Okay, maybe not every room, but several rooms. I have a basket under each bathroom sink with all of the cleaning products I use for that room. I keep wipes, glass cleaner, baking soda, and more depending on the room. It's great to have for surprise spills and saves time running back and forth for different cleaners. Don't forget a toilet brush by every toilet.

If it takes 2 minutes or less, then do it now. So many things fall into this rule and will ultimately make life easier. It can also take a lot of things off of your home cleaning schedule. For instance, cleaning my bathroom is nowhere on my home care schedule. Before you get grossed out, hear me out.

My bathrooms are always clean because I use the 2-minute rule. When I get up in the morning and am ready to shower, I spray some cleaner on my toilet, then take my shower. When I'm done with my shower but before I get out, I spray my cleaner on my shower walls and door, rinse it with my shower head, and I now have a clean shower. When I get out of the shower I give the toilet a quick scrub, wipe and flush. Clean toilet.

Then I dry my hair and get ready for my day, but before I leave the bathroom I reach under the sink, grab a wipe and wipe down the sink and counter. All clean. Total time about 4 minutes. A clean bathroom is always, priceless. If I go in just to wash my hands, I always dry my hands, wipe out the sink and any over-splash, and give the faucet a quick wipe. I find myself even doing this in public, it's become that much of a habit. Now I know this is a bit over 2 minutes, but forming that daily habit is worth the extra 4 or 5 minutes and one thing off of my home care list.

Changing your habits is another tip I have for you. One big habit I had to learn is to clean as you go. When you clean as you go, things stay more organized, and the final clean-up is minimal. The kitchen is especially great for this. When you are cooking, clean up your prep work while your meal is cooking. Rinse out the dishes you've used and put them in the dishwasher. No big pile of dirty dishes to face after cooking, and minimal dishes after you've eaten. When I'm all done in the kitchen, I grab a cleaning wipe from under the sink, give the counters, stove, and appliances a quick wipe down, and viola, a clean kitchen and one less thing on my home care list.

Realistically, my weekly home care schedule consists of mopping, vacuuming, windows, and dusting.

Thanks to the 2-minute rule and learning to change my habits, I have reduced my home care to a manageable, undaunting routine. I use these tips throughout my entire farm. When I go to feed, I grab the trusty pitchfork I have in each area and scoop the animals waste each day. It takes about 45 seconds to do this daily, rather than letting it build all week and taking 45 minutes or more to do weekly. It also takes another task off my home care list.

Design your Home Care planner to your specifications, based on your schedule, and keep it small and enjoyable. Do it with love and appreciation and you will always have a clean, welcoming home.

•FOUR•

ADDING INCOME

Whether you are looking to make an income living a self-sustained life or just reducing your expenses, at the very minimum, your projects should pay for themselves. In this chapter, we will cover this as well as how to make an actual income.

A general rule of thumb in a self-sustained life is, that everything you do must pay for itself. There are very few exceptions to this rule, but as an example, one exception I have is my horse. I call her my cheap therapy. She does provide value to my life in the relaxing rides we take and just the peace and calm of grooming her. That is her value and while she does not actually pay for herself, she is worth any expense I incur from her. Overall, though, everything must pay for itself at a minimum.

While you may not see actual dollar bills coming in, you should always see a reduction in expenses. You may not see an income from your vegetable garden, but you should see a reduction in your grocery bill.

Every year I spend about $300 on my vegetable and fruit gardens. This includes everything I need to plant, care for, harvest and preserve my vegetables and fruits. Seeds, plants, feed, ingredients for recipes, vacuum seal freezer bags, and anything else I need to grow and preserve my harvest. $300 may sound like a lot, initially, but considering that I barely have any fruits, vegetables, or sauces on my grocery list anymore, that $300 investment more than pays for itself.

The same goes for my barn cats. I spend about $300 a year on food and care for my barn cats, and while they don't bring an income, they keep the rodents off my farm and out of my animal's food, as well as other damage that rodents do chewing on things. Well worth it to me and healthier for my farm not having traps or bait all over. My cats provide no income, but they do reflect other savings in my expenses.

Then there are my dogs. My dogs are purebred LGDs or Livestock Guardian Dogs. These dogs can be spendy, but when they protect your entire livestock and farm from predators, they are more than worth it. While they do not provide an actual income, they do pay for themselves in the service they provide to my farm and there are ways to reduce their expense. Breeding is the easiest way to reduce expenses or even provide income to your bank account. I also know people who provide stud services for a fee or show them for prize money.

While I, in no way, endorse a puppy mill breeding program, I do breed any new females twice and sell the pups. I only breed them twice and that money goes directly into an account, strictly for my dogs. These dogs are guarding against large predators such as coyotes and cougars, so it's not unheard of for them to need potential vet care. That is what this account is for and to eventually replace them when they are gone. It's an account that I never want to touch, but if an emergency arises, it has been covered by the dogs, not out of my pocket.

Their food and general vaccinations do come out of my pocket, but again, more than worth it for the protection they provide.

Livestock can be a bit trickier. With livestock, you must factor in the cost of feed, bedding, and vetting. Let's use chickens as an example. You buy 10 laying hens at $5 each, that's $50. Feed for 10 hens is about $25 a month, so $300 a year. Bedding costs about $20 a month, that's about $250 a year. Your total investment per year is about $600.

Eggs are running about $6 a dozen at the local grocery store, so for your $600 investment, you could buy 100 dozen eggs at the grocery store. Do you use 100 dozen eggs for your family every year?

You have to decide for yourself what is most effective and affordable for you and your needs, but everything must pay for itself in one way or another.

Crafts are another entity in themselves. They can potentially be 100% profit. When I started with crafts, it was completely free, minus my time creating them. I sold signs that I created from old, free pallets and excess paint that I already had and they sold like crazy! From there I added throw rugs into the mix.

I started making rag rugs which are made with old T-shirts and jeans. I had lots of those around our house. Instant income with no expense. If you use what you have to start and build an income base, you can replenish your supplies inexpensively through garage sales, thrift stores, and free items in your local paper.

The first crafts that I started with free supplies helped me build an income base that allowed me to expand to my true passion of soaps, candles, and spa products. Whatever you choose and whatever your reasons for your self-sustained life, the expenses that you put in must equal what you get back, at the bare minimum.

Now to the income part of this chapter – actual income, profit in your pocket above and beyond covering the expenses.

Let's look at the vegetable gardening scenario again. You've already seen how your grocery bill can be reduced by raising your own fruits and vegetables. You are already making an income by creating savings, but let's talk about building on that and putting actual dollars in your pocket.

I grow a very large garden with a wide variety of fruits and vegetables but I have never used all of the seeds in a packet to provide for my family. That would be way too much. One year though, I decided to plant them all. I used every container and had to get pretty creative to get them all planted, but I did it. With the excess produce that I had, I gave some to friends and took the rest to our local farmers market and sold it. I had no idea how much I would make or if I would make anything, but I figured it was worth a try.

I checked out the prices at our local grocery stores and priced things a bit lower than that and went to the farmers market. No fancy packaging, no signage, nothing, and in one afternoon I made over $400. I made enough to cover my expenses for next year's garden plus profit.

I still do this. I have gotten a little fancier, added some of my crafts to my inventory, and do make more, now that I know better, what I'm doing. I try to never have expectations, except that I hope to cover next year's expenses, but I always walk away amazed at the deposit I get to make from one afternoon of work.

I don't count the time I spend raising my garden because I'm already out there raising my family's food, and there is no expense to it because I raised them from seeds that I would have wasted otherwise.

Use what you have to build your income. If you don't want to raise the produce or don't have the room, then start the excess seeds and sell them in spring as plants to sell to other gardeners.

I have a large lilac hedge in my yard. I love it but had never given it a thought except to water it in extremely hot summers. I now harvest their shoots, pot them, and sell them as lilac bushes. This can be done with virtually any of your landscape plants. Look around your place. You may be surprised at what you find.

Let's go back to the chicken and eggs example we looked at earlier in this chapter. Figuring $600 for the annual keeping of 10 hens, and odds are you aren't going to use 100 dozen eggs to make up for that investment. You could reduce your number of chickens, but I am going to show you how to make those 10 hens pay for themselves.

One way is to sell the excess eggs. Farm Fresh eggs are in high demand and prices vary depending on where you live. In my area, they go for $3-$4 per dozen. On average hens will lay an egg every day for about 6 months out of the year, depending on your climate, so that's 150 dozen a year, give or take. Let's say you use 50 of those dozens and are left with 100 dozen to sell at $4 a dozen. That's $400 income, so over half of your investment, but don't forget the 50 dozen you are using, that cost about $6 a dozen at the store. That's a grocery bill reduction of $300 a year. In total, your hens have brought in $700 and their expenses are $600 annually. That's an actual income of $100. This doesn't sound like a lot for the year, but it is still actual income. That is extra money you would not have had.

Now let me take you a step or two further in this scenario, to show you how to really expand on their income potential. The first way is to buy the right type of chicken.

In your self-sustained life, everything you do must serve at least one substantial purpose or better yet, more than one purpose. Chickens are no exception to this. When choosing which chickens to buy for your life, I highly encourage you to consider dual-purpose birds. These are hens that are great egg layers as well as great for meat. Regular laying hens are good egg birds and can be used for meat but do not grow as meaty as a dual-purpose hen. By purchasing dual-purpose hens, you are increasing the return on your investment by providing both eggs and meat for your family. This does mean you will have to buy new hens each year, but I will show you how to avoid this as well.

To increase the return on your investment even further, you can hatch chicks from some of your eggs, to sell in spring. Chicks can go for as much as $10 each versus $3 per dozen.

To do this, you will need a rooster. I know most people do not favor having roosters in their flock as they can be noisy and sometimes dangerous. I do not like keeping roosters, but I do like to hatch my chicks, so I have found somewhat of a workaround for this.

There are always roosters free in our local paper, so you can go that route if you are not concerned with cross-breeding your hens. This will not affect the egg quality. This is a great free resource if you are strictly hatching chicks to replenish your flock. If you are looking to sell your chicks, cross-breeding is not a great idea, so you may want to look at buying a rooster of the same breed as your flock. Again, look in your local paper first for the best price, but if you have a breed that is not very common in your area, plan to buy a rooster retail.

A chicken takes, on average, about 7-12 weeks to grow to meat size. Roosters can start fertilizing eggs at 4-8 months of age, depending on the breed, so they're already at butcher size when they start breeding. Use your rooster for the egg fertilization that you want or need, then you can butcher them as soon as they have fulfilled their purpose.

I have a routine for hatching out chicks, and I both sell and replenish my flocks with this method. Since I have been using this routine, I haven't purchased a single chicken, I have a continuous meat and egg supply and make an income from my chickens. Remember that everything must pay for itself, and my chickens do that on several levels.

Chickens are most productive in spring and summer. Once daylight hours reduce, so does their production. There are some ways to extend that production, but remember to give your girls a break, too. I have an abundance of eggs from my 10 hens, and there are ways to preserve eggs to get you through winter without forcing them to lay all winter.

Having said that, I keep a couple of roosters on hand, in a separate coop away from the hens. They seem to stay quieter if they can't see the hens. In August, I take a break from harvesting eggs and turn a rooster out with the hens. I let the rooster live with the hens for about 2 weeks, then I remove the rooster, take a different rooster and turn it out with the hens for the remaining 2 weeks of August. Roosters and hens will not always take to each other, so I rotate the roosters to increase the odds of fertilization.

I collect the eggs and put them into an incubator. When I remove the last rooster, I continue to collect the eggs for about 2 weeks after, for the incubator, as a hen will remain fertile for 9-14 days on average.

Most incubators have a 'candle' to see if an egg is fertile or not, and you will want to use this on each egg you add to avoid waste. Once the eggs stop showing signs of fertilization, then regular laying resumes and the incubators do the rest of the work.

Eggs will hatch between 21-25 days, and you will have your chicks. By this time, it is mid-September to early October. You will want to have an area for your chicks to safely grow.

I have two large plastic kiddie pools with heat lights suspended over half of them. The chicks will come and go from the heat as they need, so you want to make sure they can escape the heat if they want. I also have my hen coop split, so when the chicks have outgrown the pools, they can go to the coop. I split the hen coop with chicken wire so that the adult hens can see the chicks. As they grow next to the hens, they get used to each other and when they are introduced to the flock, there are little to no problems with fighting.

Hens will start laying their eggs at 18-22 weeks, so I raise my chicks all winter and they are laying in spring when people are looking to purchase chickens for eggs. This may add to the feed expense a bit, but I get more profit from layers than from the chicks themselves.

Hens lay eggs productively for about 3 years. Roosters are active breeders for about 3 years as well. Breeding your chicks allows you to replenish your flock at no cost to you, and if you have a poor layer or breeder, you can take them out of the rotation and replace them as needed.

Also, by raising my chicks all winter, I can determine which are roosters and which are laying hens. I only sell the laying hens and remember, chickens have grown to a good butchering size at 7-12 weeks. Chicken butchering happens at our farm in late winter, so by that time, I know which are roosters to be butchered and which are laying hens to be sold.

This method can be used on several livestock varieties. I have a Jersey cow which is strictly for milk, but to get milk, you must breed. I breed her every 2 years, raise her calf to butchering size, and have all of the milk I need for butter, and cheeses. Plus, I have a freezer full of beef, from butchering the calf, for less than I would have spent at the grocery store. I also have the piece of mind of knowing what my cows have eaten and no growth hormones.

I have two goats that I use for their milk to make cheese. Again, milk means breeding. Multiple births, or kids, are fairly common in goats. I have one who consistently kids twins and the other has kidded both single and twins. I know I will have at least 3 kids each time I breed, but as soon as they are weaned, I sell them. The profit from the kids pays for my goat food for the year and I get organic goat milk free.

One thing I will stress in anything you are considering selling is to use quality materials. Whether it's vegetable seeds, crafting supplies, or livestock, to command the best prices, you must offer the best quality. The livestock that I sell is all purebred. I can sell them for livestock, 4H, breeders or to show. To offer organic vegetables or plants, you must start with organic seeds.

By thinking of the multitudes of uses each item can provide, you can develop a personal blueprint to not only save money but make money in your self-sustained life.

FREE OR ALMOST FREE

Your Self-sustained life can potentially start for free. Or almost free.

Like many others, my self-sustained journey began with a garden. Growing my own food, tomatoes, specifically. I went to our local nursery and bought my tomato plants. 10 plants for $35. Not even a week later, I saw an ad for tomato plants for $1 each from a person just down the road. I could have saved $25 if I would have looked at the paper first. Lesson learned.

From that point on I started looking online and, in the paper, religiously, before going retail. It is part of my morning, 'Me Time' routine. I look at the 'Free' sections every day, whether I am looking for something specific or not. I have found free craft supplies, tools, plants, and more by doing this. I may not be looking for anything in particular, but if it's something that I will use and can get free instead of spending my hard-earned money, it's worth it.

I found all of my pallets free when I started. There are free animals. My first goat was a 5-week-old, purebred bottle baby. The owner didn't have time for a bottle baby, so she was giving it away. Please, do yourself a favor and look for free or greatly reduced prices in your local resources, before spending your money on retail.

My pressure cooker, which I still use, would have cost me over $100, but by looking at my local listings first, I found it brand new, in the box, for $45. It was a wedding gift that was never going to be used by this couple. Score!

Also, never be afraid to negotiate. That pressure cooker was listed at $55, but I asked if they would take $45 and they did. The worst that can happen is they say no. When you negotiate, lowball it a bit. I would have gladly paid $55 for the pressure cooker, but if they had said no to the $45, then I would have offered $50. A $5-$10 reduction for a sale may not be that significant to the seller, but a $5-$10 savings for you is huge when you're already looking at paying less than retail. I saved over $55 on a brand-new pressure cooker.

Free is another great way to add income to your self-sustained life. If you see something listed for free, and you know you can resell it, then jump on it! I have found free pieces of furniture that I've cleaned up, refinished, given a little TLC, and relisted for 100% profit. I am not talking about taking up a collection or to start hoarding items, but if you can do a quick turnaround on an item, for at least $10 profit, then go for it. Keep in mind the fuel it will take to go get the item as well. If you are reselling, you always want to profit at least $10.

Another almost free place to watch is the clearance section. Whether it's at a store or online, always check the clearance section. I make and sell skincare and spa products. One year I found scalp massagers on clearance for $0.25 each. I bought all of them. 100 scalp massagers for $25. I took them home and bundled them with my spa products and increased my bundle price by $8.00. For a small investment of $25, I increased my profits by $775. Total win! Always be thinking of what your personal touch can do with things.

Although money is not the most important thing, living an independent life means you always have to think about it. You have to learn to think about what to spend it on and what not to. How to make it and save it.

Myself, I don't ever want to spend my money, except on what I want. I want life on my terms, so when I want to go see a movie or travel, I go, but if I don't want to go grocery shopping or fight traffic I don't. I want to raise the majority of my food and always have full freezers and pantries. If we have a blizzard, I never want to feel I have to get somewhere until they've cleared the roads.

Use your resources to save your money. Use coupons, but only if it's something you normally use. If a rebate is more than the stamp and envelope, send it in. Shop online. If you can get an item for the same or less than you can locally, then buy it online and have it shipped to your door.

Watch for shipping charges, though. I don't buy anything online that doesn't have free shipping. Even if I have to buy a few items to get free shipping, if it's something you use regularly and you can store without spoiling, then the savings are justified.

I also do online or grocery pick up, most of the time, then I don't go into the store and impulse buy. It saves me time too. I pull up, they load my car and I'm out of there. Grocery shopping is done in 10 minutes. After all, time is money, too.

•SIX•

BUDGETING

When I first started my venture into a self-sustained life, my husband chuckled. He was supportive though and he never complained. The first thing I did was budget. I determined what I needed for my tomato plants and their care, and I estimated how much we had been spending annually on tomato-based products.

I bought my plants and some other supplies that I would need and spent $50. I planted and raised them like they were my babies. When it was harvest time, we had so many tomatoes, it was crazy! Then I spent the weekend cooking and canning spaghetti sauce. When I was all done, we had 56 quarts of sauce.

In my family, we use spaghetti sauce for something about once a week and we use the big, 2qt, jugs. They cost $8.00 each, so I figured we went through about 50 of them a year. $8x50 = $400 a year just on spaghetti sauce. Now my 56 quarts of spaghetti sauce were only about half of our annual supply, but I had just reduced our annual grocery bill by a little more than $200, for the small investment of $50. That was when I started going all out.

I started with the groceries. I made a list of every single thing that we bought regularly, from toilet paper to green beans. I went through that list and crossed off anything I couldn't make or grow. Then I budgeted what we spent on each item every year, approximately.

That's when the research started. I looked up different ways to make laundry detergent, household cleaners, and even cleaning wipes. I researched different ways to preserve foods and sampled the ways I liked to find which ones I liked best.

I started making the adjustments and as we ran out of something I replaced it with my homemade products. Our gardening season was over, so I started with household cleaners.

The very first things I changed were laundry detergent, cleaning wipes, and glass cleaner. Nobody noticed the laundry detergent or glass cleaner, but they did notice the wipes. It took a bit of getting used to, but after a couple of weeks, it was like nothing had changed.

After 6 months of changing these things, I compared our budget. For $44 I made 6 months of laundry detergent that would have normally cost $126. The cleaning wipes I made for $18 with reusable microfiber clothes. A 6-month supply would cost $16, so initially I lost $2, by purchasing the reusable microfiber cloths, but, it only costs $2 to refill the cleaning solution, so future wipes will only cost about

$4 every 6 months. My glass cleaner costs less than $1 to make a standard bottle saving me about $5 a bottle. We go through 2-3 bottles every 6 months so at the minimum, a $10 savings. Overall, by changing those 3 items, I save over $100 every 6 months. Over $200 a year savings on only 3 simple items!

Make your budget and be as detailed as you can. The more detailed you can be the more you can see where you can make changes and how much of an impact your self-sustained living can make.

After doing the budget breakdown, I started growing and preserving most of our vegetables and expanded to fruits over the years with very few exceptions. I make and preserve sauces & condiments, freeze veggies and store winter hardy produce for our annual supply. My grocery list rarely has vegetables or sauces on it.

Also, remember to budget everything. If you are raising animals, budget their feed costs. Most of my animals have corn and oats in their feedings. I used to buy these at our local feed store, in fifty-pound bags, which was costing over $100 a month. I knew I could reduce that, so I started researching and asking questions.

My neighbors who raise cattle were the answer to my prayers. They recommended that I start going straight to our grain elevator and buying the grains in bulk. Now I purchase my oats and corn by the ton. I buy a half-ton of each about every 18 months for about $400 total. Compared to the $1200 a year that I used to spend, and only making one trip for their food, it is well worth the savings.

Buying in bulk is another great way to ease the budget, if you are going to use it. Do not buy more than what you are going to use, just to save some money. Odds are that you'll end up throwing out the savings.

For instance, I buy my sugar and flour in bulk, but only once a year. I buy it during the holidays when it's at great sale prices, and I buy a lot. Then, over the winter, I bake a lot of cookies, brownies, crackers, bread, and other things to freeze for use throughout the year. The rest of the year I typically only have a simple 5-pound bag of flour and sugar. I do not want to be cooking or baking any more than I have to in the heat of summer, so I prepare for the year in winter, and that's when I stock up, and buy in bulk.

If there is a great sale on the toothpaste you use, buy your year's supply then. You know you will use it, so save the money while you can.

 Canned goods are another great thing to stock up on when there's a sale, but watch the expiration dates and only buy what you will use in that time. If your family goes through a lot of beef, consider buying half of a cow from your local butcher. The quality is usually much better and the cost is less than buying from the grocery store.

You may find you need to purchase things to store your bulk items in, such as a freezer, but in the long run, that freezer will pay for itself and be more than worth it. Look at your local garage sales and auctions, in the paper or online for storage items. I bought a dozen barrel-type shipping containers, at an estate auction, for $1.00 each, to store my feed grains in. They are perfect, air-tight, and portable. Use your imagination and the possibilities are endless.

I also grow a garden just for my animals, to help reduce food costs. I grow pumpkins, kale, sweet potatoes, and melons to supplement their diet. All of my livestock loves the pumpkin, and as a bonus, it's also a natural dewormer for them. The chickens and ducks love kale, so I grow it and freeze it up for winter when they don't get all of the fresh greens they do in summer. I do the same with the melons, and the sweet potatoes are for my dogs. I slice and dehydrate the sweet potatoes for my dog treats, at very little cost compared to buying them retail. Healthier too.

Budgeting your annual expenses will show you where your biggest expenditures are. Research ways to reduce these. Your budget will also show you the impact you're making in your self-sustained living and may entice you to take your journey further.

SAVE vs SPEND

Your decision to journey into self-sustained living is as personal and individualized as each of us is. You may be looking to save money, spare the environment, become more prepared for emergencies, all of the above, or something completely different. When I began my journey, it was strictly to save money on our grocery budget. Since then, it has grown into all of the above.

As I grew in my gardening and preserving, myself and my family started noticing the flavor of our produce was so much better. Of course, it was fresh from the garden to the table or preserved and hadn't been sitting in a warehouse for days (or longer) waiting to get to the grocery store, but it also didn't have all of the chemicals that large corporations tend to use.

For that reason, it was not only healthier for us, but for the environment as well. That got me thinking about other ways that I could make our lives healthier, be kinder to the environment, and at the same time save money.

That led me to my cleaning supplies. Behold the power of white vinegar and baking soda! Two completely natural products that are inexpensive and are the base of most of the daily cleaning supplies that you buy in the store.

Over the years, I have jumped into self-sustained living with both feet. It is second nature for me to look to myself and what I can do, before spending my hard-earned money. This is a habit that I highly recommend adopting to be successful in your self-sustained life. The more you can do yourself, or learn to do yourself, the more profitable this lifestyle will be, if only in savings.

When it comes to repair work or maintenance around my home, I always consider whether I can do it myself or not and if it's beneficial for me to do it. When I say beneficial, there are a couple of things I look at; one is time. Time is money too, so when I look at something, I figure approximately how long it would take me and determine if it's more cost-effective for me to do it or hire somebody.

Take my chimney for example. I could go buy a chimney sweep brush and probably do a good scrubbing on it to get rid of any soot and debris in there, but, I don't like heights, so I would not be comfortable or feel very secure on the roof. There also would be a lot of clean up once I was done which is a big project in itself, with soot. All of this would be at least a 4-hour project for me....at least. Calling my local chimney sweeper takes 5 minutes of my time, costs $95, and only takes him about an hour, including clean up, leaving me 4 hours to be productive somewhere else. To me, completely worth it.

The second benefit I always look for is quality and service guarantee. With my chimney sweep example, not only am I getting a thorough cleaning on the chimney, by somebody who knows what they're doing, but he also does a full inspection on the chimney, giving me peace of mind, knowing that it's solid, clean and I won't have a chimney fire.

Always weigh the benefits of hiring out a job before making that call. I can replace a gate latch, or change the oil on my vehicle but I can't confidently change a belt on my car. I do general maintenance on my vehicles, except for my daily driver. I can do the general maintenance on it, but considering that I have the oil changed, filters replaced, fluids topped off, plus brakes inspected and a tire rotation, in a half hour or less, for only $60, it's worth it to me to take it in.

I am happy to pay a professional to do the things that I don't feel confident doing or who save me significant time in my day. I have the security of knowing that a job is done correctly and I have the freedom to use my time elsewhere.

Again, time is money and you must take that into consideration as well. Fuel for your vehicle is a big one that gets overlooked. I now only drive about 4 times a month, winter, even less. I am not opposed to jumping in my car and heading off with some friends for a spontaneous outing, but when it comes to planned events, I try to coordinate errands with my outings. This is a personal choice, but I have cut my fuel budget by more than half doing this. I also can only accomplish this by staying organized.

When I do drive to town, I usually have a huge list with me. My days in town are an all-day adventure, but it's also all done when I get home. If one of the kids has a game on Saturday, then I plan all of my errands for Saturday. I make my oil change appointment, run any errands and pick up any non-perishable supplies all before the game. Go watch the game with my family and usually have lunch or supper after, then go pick up my perishables and head home.

Sometimes I stop in the mall and check out the latest fashions or home décor, whatever it is, I do it all in one trip. I am always exhausted but exhilarated after a day in town because I'm completely restocked on supplies and have dozens of new ideas for crafts, gardening, and fun in my kitchen! I have completely transformed from the spend-a-holic I was in my youth, to a person who looks at things and says, 'I can make that or do that myself'!

There are so many good tutorials out there to learn just about anything. The internet and ebooks are great for this. I love the internet for tutorials. Not only is somebody, who knows what they're doing, teaching you, but you can also see it being done.

I also take pictures of home décor, take it home and figure out how to make it. If I find it is more expensive to make, then I may purchase it on my next outing, but I almost always give myself a chance.

A few key questions to ask yourself before you part with your money:

Are there any good tutorials out there to teach me this?

Do I feel confident doing this?

Is my family's or my home's safety riding on this?

Will it take me too much time to do this?

Can I barter with a friend or neighbor for this?

If your family's safety is at stake here, always have a professional do it. If you feel confident that you can do something, then save your money and do it yourself.

If it's going to take several hours for you to do something that a professional can do in just an hour or so, weigh the savings. Your time is valuable and you can make the savings up somewhere else if the cost is within reason.

Then we come to bartering. Bartering with a friend or neighbor for services is a great way to save money. My best friend services my mower and changes the blades every fall. He's happy to do it for free, but I always bring him a case of his favorite soda as a thank you. Still cheaper than taking it to a shop, and it saved me from trying to do it and possibly breaking a spindle, which would have been much more expensive to repair.

My neighbor waters my garden if I'm out of town, and I dog-sit for her when she's out of town. Trading services is a great way to not only save money but to establish or strengthen relationships as well.

You may find, as I have, that you don't like to part with your money unless it's fun. You may be able to save for trips with your family and new things that you would like, just by thinking before you part with your money. By thinking before you buy, and relying on yourself for more, you will have very few impulse buys, more savings, and no regrets.

WHEN TO SHOP
& WHEN TO STOP

As important as it is to think about what you spend your money on, it is equally important to think about when to spend it. This is a huge area to keep in mind when you're looking to buy almost anything. A new car, appliances for your home, or even re-stocking the pantry; knowing when to shop will add up to some serious savings.

I always re-stock the pantry around Thanksgiving and Christmas. This is when the best sales are going on for all of your baking supplies and canned goods, so take advantage of the savings.

If you're buying furniture, the best times are the end of winter, mid-January, and February, and the end of summer, August, and September. This is when retailers are pushing out last season's items to bring in the new. Lots of sales; lots of savings!

Best time to buy a new car? October, November, and December. December is the very best. Dealers want to get rid of last year's models and they also have quotas to fulfill to end the year strong. It is the best time for savings on a vehicle as well as negotiating options or warranty services to the contract.

The ends of seasons are great times to save money not only on furniture, but on clothing, yard & gardening supplies, and general holiday shopping.

I always go to the store and mall the day or two after the holidays. I can get holiday décor and gifts for up to 75% off on those days, and I'm ahead of the game for next year's holidays.

I have two major shopping days in the year that I specifically save money for, and they have nothing to do with groceries or gifts. The first one is Black Friday/Cyber Monday, but not for reasons you may think.

Traditionally, I was brought up with the annual Christmas shopping weekend being Black Friday. As I grew up and had a family of my own, I realized how stressful and expensive it was to try to get the perfect gift for everybody, all in one weekend, even with great savings.

Now, there are ways around the expense of gift-giving. You can do the envelope method, where you put away x amount of dollars each payday, and that is what you have to spend on gifts. You can set a dollar amount per person and that's what you can spend on a gift. What I have found that works best for me, though, is to shop all year. No, I don't go Christmas shopping every weekend, but if, in my outings, I see something that I know somebody would like, and I can afford it, then I get it. Right then and there, I get it.

One gift down, no stress, no taxing the budget, and one name off of the list. I take it home, wrap and tag it, then stash it until Christmas. A fun fact is, sometimes I don't remember what it is, so it's just as much a surprise to me as it is to the recipient.

This has become my tradition and has evolved over the years. I now have a dedicated 'Gift Closet' and wrap the gift right away, after somebody once opened the 'Gift Closet' and saw what the gifts were. Now when I decorate my tree, the closet gets emptied and under the tree is full.

A couple of tips here:

I like to keep an even gift count for the kids, so when I take the gifts out of the closet, I make a checklist in case I need to pick up an extra for anybody.

I love the tradition of the kids making their Christmas list for Santa, so I always make sure I get one gift from their list.

Overall, though, I find this method works best for me and my budget. Feel free to adopt it, or make a method that works for you and your family.

So now you're probably wondering why I need Black Friday at all. Well, Black Friday is my Christmas gift to me. Black Friday/Cyber Monday holds exceptional savings on just about everything! There is no way I let those savings escape me. This is one of two shopping events that I use the envelope method for. I put money away all year for this event. This is the day I look for things that I want or need, that I'm not willing to pay full price for, which is almost everything!

Electronics are a big-ticket item, that I will never pay full price for, and Black Friday/Cyber Monday are just the times to get great deals on them. You may find them on sale throughout the year, but never at the savings you will find on Black Friday/Cyber Monday. It's worth the savings to wait for that purchase.

Clothing is another great savings on Black Friday. You may want a new winter coat, but if you wait a few more weeks, you can get it at up to 75% savings. Don't forget the basics either. I buy all of our pajamas, socks, jeans, and more for the year at a minimum of 50% off. Cookware, vacuums, computers...they're all on huge sales this weekend. Take advantage!

The second shopping event I specifically save for is the day or two after Christmas. I love Christmas! Everything about it from decorating, the love and kindness that always seems to be more abundant, the lights, decorating cookies, crafting, I love everything about it and the day or two after Christmas is the best time to shop for Christmas decorations, wrapping paper, next year's stocking stuffers or if you are like me, next year's color scheme.

The day or two after Christmas is also a crafters heaven for re-stocking the supplies. Ribbons, beads, glitter, and more, all at a savings of 50%-75%! What could be better? This is also a great time for finding items to re-sell.

I once went to a big chain store, the day after Christmas, and found scalp massagers that had been meant for stocking stuffers, on sale for $0.25 each. I bought 100 of them for $25, turned around and bundled them with some spa products, and increased my bundle price by $8.00. Increased profit by $775. I've also bought basic wreaths, ribbons, and decorations for 50%-75% off. I decorated the wreaths with the ribbons and decorations for about $17 for each wreath. I sold those wreaths for $65. A $48 profit, on each wreath, for the crafter in me.

The key here is to learn when the things you want or need are at their best prices and be patient.

The internet is a great research tool for this. The bigger the expense, the more research you should do. Another thing to look for is free shipping. Free Shipping has become so popular, that not only can you find the best price on the internet, but you could also save yourself time and money in fuel, by having them ship it to your front door.

Regularly used items are another thing to consider when you find great savings. If you find a great buy on something you use frequently, stock up, especially if it ships for free. Do your research and you may be surprised at the savings you can find.

MAKE THE
MOST OF YOUR TIME

Another significant impact of a self-sustained life is productivity. Like most of your self-sustained life, this is completely personal but necessary.

For this lifestyle change to have the most success, you must be productive in your chosen project. If you are growing a vegetable garden, you have to make it a priority or it will suffer and potentially die. If you are raising chickens, you must make them a priority or you will have rotten eggs in the coop and potentially sick, or worse, hens.

You must always be productive with the changes you intend to make for your self-sustained life. To do this, I again encourage you to sit back, close your eyes and envision your perfect day, week, month, and year.

Ask yourself, when is your most energetic time of day? What days have standing events in your week? Do you hate going outside in the winter? Are mornings highly active for you? Are you more active in spring than in summer? Are mid-summer days too hot and do you prefer to be inside in the air conditioning?

Write down your thoughts and answers to the questions. List all of your projects and goals. Next to them, write down what time of day or what season you like to do these things and where.

I like to be outside in the morning and early afternoon in summer, but by late afternoon or early evening, the hottest part of the day, I prefer to be inside, in my cool, air-conditioned house. Knowing this, I schedule my outside projects for the morning and early afternoon, and my indoor projects for the late afternoon.

Consider the seasons as well. We have very harsh winters where I live and I don't like to go outside if I don't have to. For that reason, I schedule most of my small crafting, making my spa products, and writing for winter.

I am also not a highly motivated person in the morning. I like to get up, have my coffee, watch the sunrise and plot my course for the day. I am a night owl though, so I put that into consideration when planning my projects. Take everything into consideration. Be honest with yourself. You want to make your projects a success, so be realistic in your scheduling.

I plan things like my canning or soap making for late, summer afternoons. I am inside in the cool of the air conditioning, but can still look out the window at the beauty of the day. I save my writing for nights when it's dark outside and I won't get sidetracked looking out the window.

Some projects require routine in your schedule, especially if you have animals, but others can be done whenever you want or wherever your schedule allows. The key is to be productive. This is your best life, so make it enjoyable and successful.

Make your schedule realistic and stick to it. If you decide you are going to do some crafting this evening, set a time and stick to it. You may find you don't feel motivated to craft at 7:00 this evening but do it anyway if that's what you've scheduled. If you don't do it, you will put it off until later, and then something else will get put off when later arrives.

Inspired or not, if you just get started, you may be surprised at how quickly motivation returns. If you wait for motivation and inspiration, you may be waiting a long time, but if you just get started, they can kick in quickly and powerfully.

Dedicate yourself to the life you are building. You chose this life, so take care of it. Even if you aren't feeling like it at the moment, just start. The rest will follow. If all you do is dream about your perfect life, it will never come. You must act.

I don't always feel like going out and lugging around hay bales for my animals, but after grudgingly putting on my boots and grabbing my gloves, I get out there and take care of them. Literally, within seconds of seeing my animals, peace comes over me and I'm petting and talking with them and enjoying my time with them. I didn't feel like doing it, but the simple step of starting changed my entire motivation and inspired me to spend more time with them, giving them a thorough checking and grooming and yes, a little extra feed, because I do love them so much.

If you're canning your garden harvest, you know that can be done day or night, but you also know that it's an end-of-summer project, so schedule it accordingly. Only you know when is the best, most productive day or time for you, so schedule carefully and for success.

Force yourself to be productive in something, each day, even when you don't feel like it. It's your responsibility to yourself, for the life you are dreaming of. Make that schedule and stick to it. If something isn't working, adjust the schedule, but do not put things off. Be productive. You'll be so much more fulfilled by your completed project than by an incomplete one.

• T E N •

SEASONAL CARE
& MAINTENANCE

Another area you will want to keep a schedule for is seasonal care and maintenance. Chapter 6 was all about budgeting and finding the areas that could make an impact on savings, so now I want to talk about the care and maintenance of your belongings. While this may not seem to be associated with your budget, there is nothing more damaging to your budget than having a surprise $800 bill come up in an emergency. Worse, an emergency that could have been avoided.

Having your furnace go out mid-winter or your house fill with smoke or fire, from a chimney that wasn't cleaned, can not only break the budget but can be potentially detrimental to you and your family.

Seasonal care and maintenance should start with a planner. Yes, one of those trustee planners that we've talked about in previous chapters.

These planners are your bibles and best friends for staying on track and organized in your self-sufficient lifestyle.

The Seasonal Care & Maintenance planner should have all of those jobs, that are not done on a regular basis, sectioned by season. Spring, Summer, Fall & Winter. This is not limited to only your home. This planner can and should include seasonal vehicle maintenance, machinery, outbuildings, yard, barn, animal shelters, and so on. Anything you can think of that only gets done once in a while.

Walk through your entire house, all buildings, sheds, yards, and gardens. No place is off limits in this planner, and don't forget gates, water spickets, and fences.

As you walk, write down anything and everything that you see that should be done. Don't worry if you think it should go into a different planner, just write it down. From there, you can make any adjustments to this or any other planner.

When I walked through my home, I wrote down everything from changing furnace filters to washing my curtains. While washing my curtains is a seasonal job, for me, it made more sense to have it in my Home Care planner.

This is your best life, so adjust to what suits your needs. Your Seasonal Care & Maintenance planner, at a minimum, should be divided by seasons, Spring, Summer, Fall, and Winter, but can also be as detailed as you want to make it. I have dividers in each season for each area of my home. I have my house, yard, garden, barn, and more. Others I have seen divide theirs up by season and month. None of this is necessary, but if it works out better for you, then do it.

Make your planner yours. Customize it to suit your needs and edit as needed. The important thing is not how you set it up, but that it is set up with everything and that you follow through with it. Emergency situations always cost more than the maintenance it takes to prevent them, so follow through with your schedules.

An example of a Seasonal Care & Maintenance planner may look something like this.

SPRING

Clean Gutters

Check/Repair Roof for Damage

Change Furnace Filters

Check Batteries in Carbon Monoxide/Fire Alarms

SUMMER

Change Furnace Filters

Run the Cleaning Cycle on the Washing Machine

Mulch Gardens

Inspect the Exterior of Buildings

Fertilize Lawn

FALL

Service Furnace & Ducts

Chimney Sweep

Winterize Plumbing

Mulch and Cover Gardens

WINTER

Check Emergency Supplies (flashlights, batteries, etc.)

Check Winter Tools and Supplies (Shovels, ice melt, etc.)

Change Furnace Filters

Clean the Backs of Appliances

This is just an example and by no means, all-inclusive, it is just to give you an idea of how to set your planner up. My seasons are about a page each and are very detailed because odds are that I would rarely think about cleaning the dust and lint off the back of my refrigerator, which could be a potential fire hazard, as well as reducing the life of the refrigerator. This planner ensures that I get everything done and checked and is safe for my family and home.

Be detailed in your walk-through and write it down. Even if it's something you want to be done, not necessarily a need, write it down. I have washing walls and outlet covers in my Spring checklist. That has nothing to do with the safety of my home, but it is a cleaning that never gets done if it's not on my list.

By keeping up on your seasonal care and maintenance, you are tackling several areas of your self-sustained life, without even knowing it. First and foremost, you are helping to prevent any costly emergencies. You are also becoming more prepared by spotting potential needs, in advance, for each season.

Imagine running low on firewood, mid-winter, and having to restock it then. It's going to be more expensive at that time of year, and you are going to be out, in the middle of winter, stacking firewood. If you had 'Check Firewood' on your Summer maintenance list, you would have replenished it then, saving money and not out stacking it in the cold of winter.

You can also become more self-reliant with these maintenance checklists. If you discover you have a leaking, outdoor faucet in Spring or Summer, you have the time to research how to fix it yourself, rather than calling an expensive plumber or having that leak turn to a break in winter, which would be very expensive.

This planner is what I call a 'Catch All' for the things that are not done regularly enough to become a habit or are not the first things on your mind. Design it accordingly and however you wish, and your home will be safe and up to your expectations, always.

Now that you have an idea of how this planner should be used, start putting yours together. Again, walk through your home, walk around the outside of your home, your yard, everywhere. Just get it all in there. You will never be sorry you have this planner.

•PROLOGUE•

Simply Self-Sustained was created to guide you successfully into your self-sustained, independent life. I hope you have found it helpful. You should now have a good idea of how to accomplish your dreams and succeed in your journey. Just follow the steps:

START SMALL - GET ORGANIZED - HAVE A BACKUP PLAN

And always remember:

DON'T BE TOO HARD ON YOURSELF – There is a learning curve to this.

MISTAKES WILL HAPPEN – They only show you how not to do something.

RESEARCH – You may learn an easier or more efficient way to do something.

THERE IS NO ONE WAY TO DO THINGS – The end result is what matters.

SCHEDULE YOUR LIFE YOUR WAY – Schedule yourself for success.

HAVE A BACK-UP PLAN – Life happens.

I wish you nothing but success, joy, and prosperity in your adventure!

Love,

Brianna

www.ingramcontent.com/pod-product-compliance
Lightning Source LLC
Chambersburg PA
CBHW031509150726
47990CB00007B/2933